Ankita Rossi

Alpe Adria Radweg
(Alpe Adria Cycle Path)

Title: Alpe Adria Radweg (Alpe Adria Cycle Path)
Author: Ankita Rossi
Published by: NEXTUNICORN PUBLISHER PROPRIETORSHIP
Publisher's Address: Shree Dwarkadhish Ji Ka Was, Emri, Rajsamand, RAJASTHAN, India. Pincode: 313342
Printer Details: Published online on various platforms.
Edition: 01
ISBN: 978-81-968306-0-1

Images Source: Pixbay: (https://pixabay.com/)

Disclaimer: The author and publisher disclaim all liability for accuracy, loss, or damage arising from the use of this travel guide; users are urged to independently verify information and prioritize personal safety.

Catalog

Welcome to the Alpe Adria Cycle Path Adventure

Unveiling the Cultural Tapestry

Join us on a captivating journey through the heart of Central Europe, where history and culture intertwine along the mesmerizing Alpe Adria Cycle Path. While Paris may boast its own unique charm, the cities that adorn this cycling route tell a distinctive tale of their own. Prepare to be enchanted as you traverse enchanting destinations like Ljubljana, Graz, and Vienna, each holding a piece of the region's rich cultural mosaic.

Ljubljana: Where Bridges Connect and Stories Unfold

Ljubljana beckons with its picturesque bridges and riverside ambiance, inviting you to immerse yourself in its cultural treasures. Marvel at the majestic Ljubljana Castle, unveil the secrets hidden within the National Gallery, and lose yourself in the vibrant local arts scene that breathes life into this captivating city.

Graz: A Harmonious Blend of Old and New

Graz stands as a testament to cultural evolution, seamlessly blending tradition with modernity. Wander through its historic Old Town, marvel at the iconic Clock Tower that stands tall as a symbol of times gone by, and indulge in contemporary art exhibitions at Kunsthaus Graz that showcase innovation at its finest.

Exploring Hidden Gems Off The Beaten Cycle Path

Venture beyond the main route for an unforgettable discovery of hidden gems awaiting intrepid explorers like you. Lose yourself in Ptuj's medieval charm or be captivated by Varazdin's Baroque wonders. And don't miss the artistic allure of Klagenfurt, a city that embraces creativity and cultural richness off the beaten cycle path.

Experience a Vivacious Lifestyle

Along the Alpe Adria Cycle Path, art effortlessly merges with daily life, creating a vivacious atmosphere that is sure to captivate your senses. This region, a cradle of creativity, has nurtured not only classical artists but also contemporary talents in music, cuisine, and design. Immerse yourself in the vibrant energy of local markets, feel the rhythm of street performances reverberating through your being, and let architectural wonders leave you spellbound.

Delight Your Palate With Gastronomic Marvels

Indulge in an epicurean journey along the Alpe Adria route and savor culinary revelations at every stop. From hearty Alpine specialties in Kranjska Gora to delicate pastries in Maribor, each bite tells a story woven with local flavors and culinary craftsmanship. Unearth hidden gems of gastronomy in Villach, relish in the fusion of Slovenian and Austrian influences in Klagenfurt's diverse culinary scene, and let your taste buds dance to the symphony of flavors this region has to offer.

Scenic Routes and Nature's Wonders

Beyond its cultural treasures lies nature's breathtaking diversity along the Alpe Adria Cycle Path. Glide through the majestic Julian Alps where pristine lakes mirror towering peaks or pedal alongside the peaceful waters of Drava River as it embraces you with its tranquility. Explore Karst landscapes that reveal subterranean wonders capable of captivating both cyclists and nature enthusiasts alike.
Embark on this remarkable cycling odyssey where every turn of your pedals unravels a new chapter within the grand tapestry weaving together culture and nature throughout the Alpe Adria region.

1. Kranjska Gora, Slovenia

Nestled in the Julian Alps, Kranjska Gora has long been a favorite destination for nature enthusiasts. It serves as a peaceful retreat and serves as an entry point to the Triglav National Park. The Vrsic Pass, a picturesque mountain pass, offers awe-inspiring panoramic views that are not to be missed. Additionally, the Jasna Lake and Planica Nordic Center are highly recommended attractions. For optimal enjoyment of outdoor activities, late spring to early fall is the ideal time to visit, while winter is perfect for skiing enthusiasts. Most attractions operate from 9 am to 6 pm. For more information or inquiries, you can reach out at +386 4 580 94 40 or visit their [Official Website](https://www.kranjska-gora.si/en).

2. Lake Bled, Slovenia

Lake Bled has a rich history that dates back to medieval times, with the majestic Bled Castle proudly perched on the cliff since 1011. One of the main attractions of Lake Bled is the enchanting Bled Island, home to the picturesque Church of the Assumption. To fully experience the beauty of Lake Bled, taking a Pletna boat ride is an absolute must. For optimal weather conditions, it is recommended to visit during late spring to early fall. If you plan on visiting Bled Castle, keep in mind that it generally opens its doors from 8 am to 8 pm. For more information or inquiries, you can contact them at +386 4 578 05 00 or visit their official website at [Official Website](https://www.bled.si/en/).

3. Ljubljana, Slovenia

Ljubljana's fascinating history can be traced back to its Roman origins, and the medieval Old Town stands as a testament to its rich heritage. When exploring this captivating city, be sure to visit iconic attractions such as Ljubljana Castle, the Triple Bridge, and Preseren Square. To fully experience the charm of Ljubljana, take a relaxing boat tour along the picturesque Ljubljanica River. Whether you choose to visit during the vibrant summer festivals or any other time of the year, there is always something exciting happening in this lively city. Ljubljana Castle is open from 9 am to 9 pm for those eager to explore its historical wonders. For more information and inquiries, you can contact +386 1 306 12 15 or visit their [Official Website](https://www.visitljubljana.com/en/).

4. Klagenfurt, Austria

Klagenfurt, with its origins dating back to the 12th century, has a captivating history that showcases the vibrant influences of the Renaissance era. One of its prominent attractions is the Lindwurm Dragon monument, which can be found at Neuer Platz. For those who enjoy shopping, the City Arkaden shopping district offers a delightful experience. To fully immerse in the city's charm, it is recommended to visit during spring and summer when outdoor events and festivals take place. Museums and other attractions usually open their doors from 10 am to 6 pm, allowing visitors ample time to explore. For further information or inquiries, you can contact +43 463 537 2222 or visit their [Official Website](https://www.visitklagenfurt.at/en).

5. Villach, Austria

Villach has a rich history that dates back more than a thousand years, showcasing a blend of Austrian and Italian influences. When exploring the city, make sure to visit some of its key attractions such as the Drau River promenade, Villach Old Town, and the scenic Villach Alpine Road. For the best experience, plan your trip during the summer when you can enjoy outdoor activities and vibrant events. Most local attractions open their doors from 9 am to 6 pm. If you need any further information or assistance, feel free to contact +43 4242 205 2900 or visit the official website at https://www.villach.at/en.

Dobbiaco, nestled in the breathtaking Dolomites, has a rich history dating back to the Roman era. This picturesque town seamlessly combines Alpine charm with Italian influences, creating a unique and captivating atmosphere.

One of the main highlights of Dobbiaco is Toblach Lake, a serene body of water that offers a tranquil escape for visitors. The stunning Tre Cime di Lavaredo, with their majestic peaks, provide an awe-inspiring backdrop for nature enthusiasts and hikers alike. Additionally, Gustav Mahler's composing cabin adds a touch of cultural significance to the town.

To fully enjoy Dobbiaco's natural beauty and outdoor activities, it is recommended to visit during late spring to early fall when the weather is pleasant and inviting. During this time, hiking trails are open and beckon adventurers to explore the surrounding landscapes.

When planning your visit, keep in mind that local attractions typically operate from 9 am to 5 pm. This ensures ample time to immerse yourself in Dobbiaco's offerings and make the most of your experience.

For more information or inquiries, you can reach out to Dobbiaco at +39 0474 972 132. Alternatively, you can visit their official website at [Official Website](https://www.dobbiaco.info/en/) for additional details and resources.

Immerse yourself in the enchanting history and natural wonders of Dobbiaco as you embark on an unforgettable journey through this captivating destination.

7. Cortina d'Ampezzo, Italy

Cortina has a fascinating history, starting as a Roman trading post and evolving into a popular winter sports destination. Its attractions include the Olympic Ice Stadium, Tofana di Rozes, and the pedestrianized Corso Italia. If you're planning a visit, winter is perfect for skiing while summer offers opportunities for hiking and mountain biking. The opening hours of the attractions may vary, but they typically open from 9 am to 7 pm. For more information, you can contact them at +39 0436 869086 or visit their official website at [Official Website](https://www.cortina.dolomiti.org/en/).

8. Tarvisio, Italy

Tarvisio has a rich history, thanks to its strategic position where Italy, Austria, and Slovenia intersect. This unique location has shaped the town's past. When you visit Tarvisio, there are several key attractions that you shouldn't miss out on. The Fusine Lakes, Mount Lussari, and the Sanctuary of Mount Lussari are among the top highlights. These attractions offer breathtaking natural beauty and opportunities for outdoor activities such as skiing in winter and hiking in summer.

If you plan to explore Tarvisio's local attractions, keep in mind that they typically open their doors from 9 am to 6 pm. It's good to know this information so you can plan your visit accordingly. For any inquiries or additional details, you can contact +39 0428 2396 or visit the official website at https://www.turismofvg.it/Tarvisio.

Tarvisio truly offers a remarkable experience throughout the year with its diverse range of activities and scenic wonders. Whether you prefer winter sports or summer adventures, this charming town has something for everyone. So pack your bags and get ready for an unforgettable journey in Tarvisio!

9. Ferlach, Austria

Ferlach, also known as the "Town of Gunsmiths," has a rich history that revolves around its long-standing tradition of gun-making. This history is deeply ingrained in the fabric of the town.

When visiting Ferlach, there are several key attractions worth exploring. The Ferlach Museum offers a glimpse into the town's past, while St. Stefan Church showcases stunning architecture and religious significance. Additionally, the historic market square is a hub of activity and charm.

To make the most of your visit, it is recommended to plan your trip during spring and summer. These seasons offer pleasant weather and an array of outdoor events and festivals to enjoy.

When it comes to visiting museums and attractions in Ferlach, they typically adhere to opening hours from 10 am to 5 pm. This allows visitors ample time to explore and immerse themselves in the local culture.

For any inquiries or further information, you can contact +43 4227 2316 or visit the [official website](https://www.ferlach.at/en/).

10. Maribor, Slovenia

Maribor, a town with a long and fascinating history dating back to Roman times and influenced by the medieval era, holds great allure. Its key attractions include Maribor Castle, Old Vine House, and the Lent district situated along the picturesque Drava River. To witness the blooming vineyards, late spring is an ideal time to visit, while summer offers vibrant festivals. The opening hours of these attractions typically span from 9 am to 6 pm. For more information or inquiries, you can contact them at +386 2 234 66 11 or visit their official website at [Official Website](https://www.visitmaribor.si/en/).

Ptuj is a town with a rich history that dates back thousands of years, making it one of the oldest towns in Slovenia. Its historical significance is evident through the influence of Roman and medieval eras.

When exploring Ptuj, there are several key attractions worth mentioning. The Ptuj Castle stands as a prominent landmark, along with the Orpheus Monument, both offering glimpses into the town's past. Additionally, the old town exudes an atmospheric charm that captivates visitors.

To make the most of your visit, it is recommended to plan your trip during the summer months. This time of year is particularly vibrant due to the carnival festivities and cultural events that take place.

If you're wondering about opening hours for various attractions in Ptuj, they generally operate from 10 am to 5 pm.

For further information or inquiries, you can reach out to +386 2 779 60 11 or visit their [Official Website](https://www.ptuj.info/en/).

Varazdin, with its stunning Baroque architecture, serves as a testament to its fascinating past as a former capital of Croatia. The city boasts an array of magnificent palaces, picturesque churches, and delightful squares that showcase its rich history.

When exploring Varazdin, make sure to visit some of its key attractions such as Varazdin Castle, St. John the Baptist Church, and the beautiful King Tomislav Square. These landmarks offer a glimpse into the city's cultural heritage and architectural splendor. To make the most of your visit, plan your trip during late spring or early fall when the weather is pleasant and ideal for outdoor exploration.

The opening hours of Varazdin's attractions typically range from 9 am to 6 pm. This allows visitors ample time to immerse themselves in the beauty and history that this charming city has to offer.

For more information or inquiries about Varazdin and its attractions, you can contact +385 42 214 511. Additionally, you can visit the official website [here](https://www.tourism-varazdin.hr/en/).

Let yourself be captivated by Varazdin's captivating charm and immerse yourself in its rich history during your visit!

13. Zagreb, Croatia

Zagreb, the capital of Croatia, holds a rich historical significance with its enchanting Upper Town that dates back to medieval times. This part of the city showcases a harmonious blend of Austro-Hungarian influences, adding to its allure.

When exploring Zagreb, make sure to visit St. Mark's Church, Zagreb Cathedral, and the bustling Tkalciceva Street. These attractions offer a glimpse into the city's cultural and architectural heritage.

No matter when you plan your visit, Zagreb has something to offer year-round. During winter, the city comes alive with vibrant Christmas markets that add an extra layer of charm.

The opening hours of various attractions may vary, but generally speaking, they are open from 9 am to 6 pm. It's always a good idea to check specific timings before planning your itinerary.

For more information and assistance, you can contact +385 1 48 48 021 or visit the official website [here](https://www.infozagreb.hr/&lang=en).

Celje has a rich history that is closely connected to its medieval castle, which dates back to the 13th century. This castle offers breathtaking views of the city. In addition to the castle, other notable attractions in Celje include the Old Counts' Mansion and the historic Old Town. If you're planning a visit, it's recommended to come during the summer when you can experience cultural events and festivals. The attractions in Celje typically open at 10 am and close at 6 pm. For more information, you can contact +386 3 428 79 36 or visit their [Official Website](https://www.celje.si/en/).

Bad Radkersburg, with its rejuvenating thermal spas, has a rich history dating back to the 14th century, drawing in visitors thanks to its healing waters. The town offers a range of attractions, including the renowned Bad Radkersburg Spa, the charming Old Town, and the picturesque City Park. Whether you're seeking a relaxing spa retreat or outdoor activities, Bad Radkersburg is a year-round destination with something for everyone. The opening hours of the spa and wellness facilities may vary, but they generally operate from 9 am to 7 pm. For more information and bookings, you can contact +43 3476 2545 or visit their [Official Website](https://www.badradkersburg.at/en).

Graz, a city recognized as a UNESCO World Heritage site, has a captivating history that can be traced back to the Roman era. Its architectural splendor spans from the Renaissance period to modern times, leaving behind a remarkable legacy.

Among the notable attractions in Graz are Eggenberg Palace, Graz Art Museum, and the Murinsel—an enchanting island nestled within the Mur River.

To make the most of your visit, it is recommended to plan it during spring and summer when outdoor events and festivals take place in abundance. During these seasons, you can immerse yourself in the vibrant atmosphere and enjoy various cultural celebrations.

When exploring Graz's museums and attractions, keep in mind that they typically open their doors from 10 am to 6 pm. This allows visitors ample time to appreciate the rich cultural heritage on display.

For further information or inquiries, you can reach out to +43 316 8075 0 or visit their [Official Website](https://www.graztourismus.at/en).

Murau, situated in the enchanting Mur Valley, boasts vibrant facades and an ambiance that takes you back to the medieval era.

Its rich history traces back to the 13th century, adding a touch of authenticity to its charm.

One of the main highlights of Murau is its magnificent castle, which stands as a testament to its past. Additionally, don't miss out on exploring the renowned Murau Brewery and immersing yourself in the beauty of Murau's Old Town.

To make the most of your visit, plan your trip during the summer season when you can enjoy outdoor activities and partake in cultural events that showcase the spirit of this captivating destination.

When it comes to operating hours, most attractions in Murau are open from 9 am to 5 pm, ensuring ample time for exploration and discovery.

For any inquiries or further information, you can reach out to +43 3532 2530 or visit their [Official Website](https://www.murau.at/en/).

18. Judenburg, Austria

Judenburg exudes its medieval allure through the impeccably maintained structures that have stood the test of time, such as the magnificent St. Nikolaus Church, which traces its origins back to the 12th century.

One of the main highlights is the bustling Hauptplatz square, where you can immerse yourself in the vibrant city atmosphere. Additionally, don't miss out on exploring the Judenburg Planet Trail and marveling at the grandeur of Judenburg Castle.

To fully experience all that Judenburg has to offer, it is recommended to visit during the summer months when the city comes alive with cultural events and a lively ambiance.

Most attractions in Judenburg typically operate from 10 am to 5 pm, providing ample time for exploration and enjoyment. For further information or inquiries, you can contact +43 3572 830 37 or refer to their [Official Website](https://www.judenburg.com/en/).

Here's what you need to know for your Alpe Adria Cycle Path adventure:

Currency:

- As you travel through Slovenia, Austria, and Italy along the Alpe Adria Cycle Path, you'll encounter different currencies. Slovenia and Austria both use the Euro (€), while Italy uses the Slovenian Tolar. Make sure to have the appropriate currency for each leg of your journey, and you can find ATMs in towns and cities for convenience.

Language:

- Along the Alpe Adria Cycle Path, you'll come across different languages. Slovenian is spoken in Slovenia, German in Austria, and Italian in Italy. While English may be spoken in tourist areas, knowing basic phrases in each language can enrich your cultural interactions and make your cycling experience more immersive.

Useful Websites:

- To make the most of your journey on the Alpe Adria Cycle Path, check out these online resources:

  - Slovenian Railways (www.slo-zeleznice.si): Provides train travel information in Slovenia.

  - Austrian National Tourist Office (www.austria.info): Explore tourist attractions in Austria.

  - Italian Tourism (www.italia.it): Italy's official tourism website with comprehensive travel information.

  - EuroVelo (www.eurovelo.com): Details about EuroVelo 7 route that includes the Alpe Adria Cycle Path.

Daily Costs:

Budget (Less than €100):

- There are budget-friendly options along the Alpe Adria Cycle Path. Hostels offer dorm beds for €15-30, while budget hotel rooms range from €50 to €110. You can find affordable meals at local eateries with prices typically between €6 and €12 for pizza or pasta dishes.

Midrange (€100–€250):

- If you're looking for more comfort during your journey on the Alpe Adria Cycle Path, there are midrange options available. Double rooms in midrange hotels range from €110 to €200. Enjoy local restaurants with meals priced at approximately €25 to €50 per person. Admission to attractions usually ranges from €4 to €15.

Top End (More than €250):

- For travelers seeking luxury experiences, there are options along the Alpe Adria Cycle Path. Four- or five-star hotel rooms range from €200 to €450. Indulge in top-end restaurants with prices between €50 and €150 per person. Cultural experiences, such as opera performances, may cost between €40 and €200.

Opening Hours:

- Keep in mind that opening hours vary along the Alpe Adria Cycle Path. High-season hours usually apply from April to September or October, while low-season hours are in effect from October or November to March. Note that hours may decrease during the shoulder and low seasons.

- Here are some general opening hours:
  - Banks: Monday to Friday, 8:30am–1:30pm and 3:30–4:30pm
  - Restaurants: Noon–2:30pm and 7:30–11pm or midnight
  - Cafes: 7:30am–8pm
  - Bars and clubs: 10pm–4am
  - Shops: Monday to Saturday, 9am–1pm and 4–8pm

Arriving along the Alpe Adria Cycle Path:

- Depending on where you start your journey, major airports include Ljubljana Jože Pučnik Airport in Slovenia, Klagenfurt Airport in Austria, and Venice Marco Polo Airport in Italy. You can easily reach city centers from these airports via trains, buses, and taxis.

With these practical details at hand, embark on your Alpe Adria Cycle Path adventure confidently. Immerse yourself in the breathtaking landscapes, diverse cultures, and delightful cycling experiences along the way.

Embark on a Thrilling Cycling Adventure Along the Alpe Adria Cycle Path - 2 Weeks

Discover the Enchanting Alpe Adria Region

From Day 1 to Day 3, set off on your cycling odyssey in the enchanting Alpine town of Kranjska Gora, surrounded by majestic mountains. Immerse yourself in the pristine landscapes and prepare for your exciting journey ahead. Make sure to explore Lake Jasna, take a cable car ride to the Vitranc slopes, and bask in the serene ambiance of this picturesque destination.

Moving on to Day 4 to Day 6, pedal your way towards the iconic Lake Bled in Slovenia. Marvel at the medieval castle perched atop a cliff and be captivated by a charming island nestled in the middle of the lake. Don't miss out on visiting Bled Castle, hopping aboard a traditional pletna boat to Bled Island, and relishing in breathtaking views of the Julian Alps.

Continue your adventure from Day 7 to Day 9 as you head towards Ljubljana, Slovenia's vibrant capital city. Delight in its lively atmosphere along the Ljubljanica River and get lost in its historic Old Town. Take time to explore Ljubljana Castle and immerse yourself in the city's rich cultural offerings while enjoying leisurely rides along its numerous cycling paths.

Crossing over into Austria on Day 10 to Day 12, discover Villach, a charming town nestled along the Drau River. Experience an intriguing blend of Austrian and Italian influences as you wander through historic squares and soak up alpine charm that defines this picturesque destination.

As you reach Dobbiaco on Day 13 to Day 15 and traverse into Italy, prepare yourself for breathtaking landscapes surrounded by Dolomites' grandeur. Immerse yourself in cultural richness as you explore Tre Cime di Lavaredo, cycle along the Drava River, and embrace the unique blend of Italian and Austrian cultures.

On Day 16 to Day 18, find yourself cycling through the captivating Ampezzo Valley towards Cortina d'Ampezzo. This charming town is renowned for its winter sports and alpine beauty, offering a plethora of outdoor adventures and cultural experiences. Make sure to explore the Tofane Mountains, visit the Olympic Ice Stadium, and soak in the enchanting atmosphere that surrounds you.

Concluding your cycling adventure on Day 19 to Day 21 in Tarvisio, Italy, experience a fascinating blend of Italian, Austrian, and Slovenian influences set against a captivating mountain backdrop. Explore Fusine Lakes, discover the scenic beauty of Fusine in Valromana, and indulge in panoramic views of the Julian Alps. With a sense of accomplishment and cherished memories in tow, bid farewell to this incredible journey.

Practical Tips:

- Terrain: The Alpe Adria Cycle Path offers diverse terrain with varying landscapes from mountains to valleys. Ensure your bike is suitable for different conditions.

- Accommodations: Plan your overnight stays at cyclist-friendly accommodations along the route. Choose from cozy guesthouses to bike-friendly hotels.

- Cuisine: Delight in the local culinary delights offered by each region. From hearty Slovenian dishes to Italian delicacies, savor regional wines and specialties as part of your gastronomic adventure.

Embark on this exhilarating cycling journey through the Alpe Adria region where every pedal stroke reveals new facets of natural beauty and cultural richness. Embrace the freedom of open roads and immerse yourself in thrilling exploration within this enchanting cycling paradise.

Embarking on Hiking Escapades

Location: Stelvio National Park, Italy

Immerse yourself in the awe-inspiring landscapes of the Dolomites as you venture into Stelvio National Park in Italy. Prepare to be captivated by breathtaking vistas, serene lakes, and enchanting trails that cater to every hiking preference.

Location: Villach, Austria

Get ready for an exhilarating hiking adventure in Villach, Austria, where the surrounding Alpine landscapes offer a diverse range of trails suitable for all skill levels. Explore the town's historical charm and soak in panoramic views of the region.

Thrilling Water Adventures Await

Location: Lakes of Bled and Bohinj, Slovenia

Embark on a paddling escapade along the crystal-clear waters of Slovenia's renowned lakes, including the iconic Lake Bled and Lake Bohinj. Take a refreshing swim amidst the stunning alpine scenery that surrounds you.

Location: Drau River, Villach, Austria

For water enthusiasts seeking both tranquility and excitement, kayaking down the picturesque Drau River is an absolute must. Immerse yourself in lush landscapes as you navigate this scenic waterway in Villach, Austria.

Discovering Majestic Mountains

Location: Julian Alps, Slovenia

Unleash your adventurous spirit as you venture into the majestic Julian Alps. Cycle through Dobbiaco in Italy and explore charming alpine towns along your journey. Marvel at panoramic views, conquer mountainous terrains with ease, and savor a unique blend of cultures along the way.

Location: Dolomites, Italy

Experience cycling like never before as you traverse through the iconic Dolomites. These magnificent mountains offer challenging routes for rock climbing enthusiasts while treating everyone to breathtaking vistas at every turn. Brace yourself for unforgettable vie ferrate experiences in the Brenta Dolomites.

Indulging in Culinary Delights

Location: Local Eateries in Villach, Austria

Delight your taste buds with the alpine charm of Austrian cuisine in Villach. Explore the local eateries and indulge in traditional dishes that showcase the rich flavors unique to this cultural crossroads.

Location: Italian Gastronomy in the Dolomites

As you cycle through the picturesque Dolomites, prepare to be tantalized by the diverse flavors of Italian gastronomy. Each stop along your route unveils a culinary tapestry that invites you to savor regional specialties and embark on a true culinary adventure.

Choosing Your Optimal Time

- April to June: Immerse yourself amidst blooming wildflowers as you embark on cycling and hiking adventures.

- July to September: Enjoy perfect weather for water activities and other warm-weather adventures.

- Late Spring and Early Summer: Optimal temperatures make it an ideal time for mountainous expeditions, allowing you to fully appreciate the breathtaking landscapes.

Prepare yourself for an extraordinary journey along the Alpe Adria Cycle Path. Each location along this remarkable route offers a seamless blend of natural beauty, cultural richness, and thrilling activities that will leave you with unforgettable memories. Get ready to embark on an adventure like no other!

A brief History of Alpe Adria Path

The Alpe Adria Path, a testament to the rich tapestry of history woven across the Alpine and Adriatic regions, has its origins deeply rooted in ancient times. These paths, which now form the Alpe Adria trail, were once traveled by ancient civilizations. This historical legacy echoes through the ages.

In ancient times, before the Roman era, these paths served as vital trade routes connecting Mediterranean cultures with Alpine settlements. Traders, merchants, and travelers journeyed through rugged terrains, exchanging goods, ideas, and cultural influences. Along the path today, remnants of ancient settlements and artifacts tell tales of a bygone era where knowledge and resources shaped the destiny of these lands.

As the Roman Empire expanded its reach, these routes became even more strategically important. The Romans were known for their engineering prowess and constructed roads that stretched across the Alps to facilitate trade and communication. The well-preserved remnants of ancient roads and settlements along the Alpe Adria Path still bear witness to Roman footsteps.

After the decline of the Roman Empire came a period of transformation as various medieval powers vied for control over the region. Feudal lords rose and fell along this path while medieval trade routes were established. Fortifications stand as silent sentinels to remind us of this turbulent history.

During the Renaissance period in Europe, which followed the Middle Ages, there was a renewed interest in these ancient paths along with an artistic and intellectual resurgence in the Alpe Adria region. Scholars, artists,and thinkers traversed this trail seeking inspiration from landscapes that had witnessed history's ebb-and-flow.

The cities along the Alpe Adria Path became vibrant centers for artistic exchange during this time. Florence attracted famous figures like Leonardo da Vinci,Michelangelo,and Botticelli who left an indelible mark on Italian culture.The cultural efflorescence extended beyond Italy,introducing new influences throughoutthe entire region covered bytheAlpeAdriatrail.

The Habsburg Monarchy, a powerful force in Central Europe during the Renaissance, played a significant role in shaping the political and cultural landscape of the Alpe Adria region. Their influence can be seen in the architecture, governance, and traditions of cities along the path. The art, architecture, and historical landmarks that grace the Alpe Adria trail are a testament to this cultural resurgence.

As modernity arrived with the industrial revolution, profound changes occurred intheAlpeAdriaregion.The once-pristine paths that witnessed traders and Renaissance thinkers were now impacted by railways and highways.Modern transportation infrastructure brought both progress and challenges totheAlpeAdriaPath.

The rise of nation-states inthe19th century further alteredthepolitical dynamics of theregion.The AlpeAdriatrail crossed national borders marked by distinct identities. Political shifts reshapedthecourseofhistoryintheAlpeAdriaregion,suchasItaly's unificationandthedissolutionofempires.

Despite these changes,theAlpeAdriaPath continuedto serve asaculturalconduit.Architectural wonders influenced by Art NouveauandJugendstil movements adorned cities alongthetrail.While adapting to changing times,the path retained its historical essence.Some sections preservetheancient roads asatestamenttotheregion's enduring spirit amidstthemodern strains it faced.

The Alpe Adria Path has experienced a remarkable resurgence in recent times, becoming more than just a historical relic and transforming into an exciting trail that captivates modern-day adventurers. The late 20th and early 21st centuries have witnessed a renewed interest in sustainable tourism, outdoor recreation, and cultural exploration, which has thrust the Alpe Adria Path back into the limelight.

A significant chapter in the path's modern history is the creation of the Alpe Adria Trail. This long-distance hiking and cycling route stretches across Austria, Slovenia, and Italy, symbolizing transnational collaboration, environmental stewardship, and a celebration of the region's cultural diversity. Its establishment in 1977 marked a turning point for the path.

Travelers embarking on the Alpe Adria Path today are greeted with a harmonious blend of ancient history and contemporary vitality. The trail meanders through landscapes that have witnessed centuries of human endeavors, connecting cities that resonate with echoes from both medieval times and the Renaissance era. It caters not only to outdoor enthusiasts but also to cultural explorers who are eager to dive into the layered narratives of this captivating region.

As time goes on, the Alpe Adria Path continues to evolve while remaining a testament to the enduring spirit of its surrounding lands. The trails themselves bear witness to rich history that acts as a guide for those seeking more than just physical beauty but also an immersive experience encompassing culture, history, and ecology unique to the Alpe Adria region.

1. Mountain Huts in the Alpine Splendor

As cyclists traverse the breathtaking Alpine stretches of the Alpe Adria Path, they come across a network of charming mountain huts, known as rifugi, that offer a rustic yet authentic lodging experience. These refuges, open from July to September, provide accommodation in dormitories that capture the communal spirit of mountain life. Some larger rifugi even offer double rooms for a more private stay. It's advisable to make reservations in advance due to limited availability and the path's popularity during the summer months. Prices range from €20 to €30 per person, including breakfast, with an additional charge of €10 to €15 for dinner. The Club Alpino Italiano (CAI) operates many of these mountain huts, ensuring a reliable and welcoming haven for weary cyclists.

2. Bed and Breakfasts: A Charming Respite

As cyclists pedal through picturesque landscapes along the Alpe Adria Cycle Path, they will come across delightful Bed and Breakfasts (B&Bs) scattered across both urban and rural settings. From lovingly restored farmhouses to quaint seaside bungalows, these B&Bs offer a personalized and intimate lodging experience. Prices per person vary between €30 to €100, catering to different budgets. For comprehensive information on available B&Bs that reflect local character and hospitality, cyclists can visit Bed & Breakfast Italia (www.bbitalia.it), which serves as a valuable resource.

3. Cycling Oasis: Campgrounds Along the Path

For those seeking a closer connection with nature, the Alpe Adria Cycle Path provides access to various campgrounds that offer both convenience and tranquility amidst outdoor splendor. Equipped with amenities such as swimming pools, restaurants, and supermarkets; these campgrounds are an excellent choice for cyclists who prefer a more relaxed and communal setting. Campgrounds are categorized by star ratings, and prices vary with the season, peaking during July and August. Websites like

Campeggi.com, Camping.it, and Italcamping.it provide comprehensive lists of campgrounds, empowering cyclists to strategically plan their outdoor stays.

4. Monastic Serenity: Convents and Monasteries

The Alpe Adria Cycle Path presents a unique accommodation option in the form of convents and monasteries. While some prioritize pilgrims or individuals on spiritual retreats, many open their doors to tourists, offering a serene and budget-friendly lodging experience. Although there may be early curfews in place, the reasonable prices and distinctive atmosphere make convents and monasteries an enticing choice. Platforms such as MonasteryStays.com, In Italy Online, and Chiesa di Santa Susanna provide options for travelers to explore these cultural-rich accommodations along their cycling adventure.

5. Hostels: Budget-Friendly Haven for Cyclists

Catering to the budget-conscious traveler, hostels or "ostelli per la gioventù," affiliated with Hostelling International (HI), offer an affordable yet sociable lodging option. To stay at associated youth hostels in Italy, a valid HI card is required. These accommodations typically provide dormitory beds with nightly rates ranging from approximately €16 to €30 including a buffet breakfast. Single and double rooms are also available at slightly higher prices, providing cyclists with an affordable and communal atmosphere to rest and recharge along the Alpe Adria Cycle Path.

6. Homely Retreats: Rental Accommodations

For cyclists planning an extended stay or seeking a more private retreat, rental accommodations offer a viable choice. While finding short-term leases in major cities can be challenging and may come at a premium price; various websites like Guest in Italy, Homelidays, and Interhome offer an array of rental accommodations throughout Italy. Travelers can explore options that suit their preferences, from small apartments near city centers to shared student flats, providing a sense of home away from home.

Exploring the Alpe Adria Cycle Path requires a deep understanding of visa and residency regulations to ensure a smooth and compliant journey. Here's a comprehensive guide to the relevant requirements for travelers embarking on this scenic route:

1. Schengen Treaty for European Citizens:

   - European citizens from Schengen Treaty countries can freely enter Italy using a valid identity card or passport. The ease of travel showcases the seamless borders within the Schengen Zone.

2. Visa Exemptions for Select Countries:

   - Visitors from 28 non-EU countries, including Australia, Brazil, Canada, Israel, Japan, New Zealand, and the USA, enjoy visa exemptions for tourist stays of up to 90 days. It's important to note that visa requirements may vary for those planning to venture into the UK and Ireland.

3. Visas for Non-EU and Non-Schengen Nationals:

   - Non-EU and non-Schengen nationals who plan to stay in Italy for more than 90 days or have purposes beyond tourism (such as study or work) may require specific visas.

   - For detailed and up-to-date visa requirements, travelers can refer to the official website www.esteri.it/visti/home_eng.asp or contact an Italian consulate.

4. Residence and Work for EU Citizens:

   - EU citizens, benefiting from freedom of movement, can reside and work in Italy without permits. However, after three months of continuous stay, registration at the municipal registry office is mandatory. Proof of employment or sufficient financial means may be requested.

5. Permanent Residence for Non-EU Foreign Citizens:

   - Non-EU foreign citizens who have legally resided in Italy uninterrupted for five years can apply for permanent residency.

   Permesso di Soggiorno (Permit to Stay):

- Non-EU citizens planning a stay longer than one week at a single address should obtain a 'permesso di soggiorno' from the local police station. It's worth noting that tourists staying in hotels are usually exempt from this requirement.

- Acquiring a 'permesso di soggiorno' is crucial for extended stays, work, or study, involving a detailed application process and specific documentation. However, EU citizens are exempt from this requirement.

Study Visas:

- Non-EU citizens who wish to study at an Italian educational institution must apply for a study visa at the nearest Italian embassy or consulate.

- The application process typically includes providing proof of enrollment, paying fees, and demonstrating sufficient financial resources for the duration of studies. Study visas align with the study period and can be renewed within Italy based on continued enrollment and financial stability.

Understanding and following these visa and residency intricacies ensures that travelers along the Alpe Adria Cycle Path navigate legalities seamlessly. Always verify the latest requirements through official channels to have a trouble-free and enriching travel experience.

Embarking on a journey along the Alpe Adria Cycle Path unveils a world teeming with diverse landscapes and captivating cultural experiences. This scenic route is a year-round destination for cycling enthusiasts, with each season bringing its own set of highlights. Let's dive into the wonders awaiting travelers throughout the year:

Spring (March to May):

- Nature's Awakening: As spring unfolds, witness Mother Nature coming to life along the path. Lush greenery, vibrant wildflowers, and blossoming trees create a picturesque backdrop, especially in regions like Carinthia and Friuli Venezia Giulia.

- Perfect Weather: Enjoy cycling in pleasant temperatures ranging from 10 to 20 degrees Celsius, providing an ideal climate for exploring without sweltering under the summer heat.

Summer (June to August):

- Long Days of Exploration: With the summer solstice bringing extended daylight hours, cyclists have ample time to discover charming towns, picturesque lakeshores, and cultural landmarks along their journey.

- Festivals and Local Flair: Immerse yourself in the lively atmosphere of summer festivals held in towns and villages along the way. These festivities offer a glimpse into local traditions through music, culinary delights, and more.

- Alpine Bliss: Traverse through breathtaking alpine sections of the path while relishing spectacular views of towering peaks and pristine lakes under the warm embrace of summer.

Autumn (September to November):

- A Tapestry of Colors: Cycle through nature's palette as autumn paints landscapes with vibrant hues. The wooded sections of the path transform into mesmerizing tapestries adorned with shades of reds, oranges, and golds in places like Julian Alps and Austrian countryside.

- Harvest Festivities: Engage in region-specific harvest celebrations where you can sample freshly picked fruits, local wines, and seasonal culinary delights in the vineyard-rich areas.

Winter (December to February):

- A Winter Wonderland: Embrace the enchanting winter charm as snow blankets the northern sections of the route, turning it into a serene wonderland. Explore the path's beauty against the backdrop of snow-capped peaks.

- Cozy Alpine Villages: Experience the warmth and coziness of alpine villages along the way. Indulge in hearty local cuisine and perhaps even witness traditional winter celebrations.

Year-round Highlights:

- Cultural Gems: Regardless of the season, immerse yourself in the rich cultural heritage found in towns like Salzburg, Udine, and Grado. These destinations boast unique historical sites and architectural wonders that will transport you through time.

- Delicious Discoveries: Delight your taste buds with local flavors throughout the year. From indulging in Alpine specialties in Austria to savoring Mediterranean-inspired dishes in Italy, each region offers its own gastronomic treasures. Seasonal produce adds a delightful dimension to your culinary journey.

Whether you are captivated by spring blooms, enchanted by sun-soaked summer days, mesmerized by autumn's colorful landscapes, or drawn to winter's tranquility, one thing is certain—the Alpe Adria Cycle Path promises an unforgettable adventure throughout all seasons. Each chapter paints a distinctive portrait that invites cyclists to savor the ever-changing beauty of this remarkable route.

Are you ready for an exhilarating adventure along the Alpe Adria Cycle Path? This cycling route offers diverse landscapes and breathtaking views, but safety and preparedness should be your top priorities. To ensure a smooth and enjoyable journey, here are some practical tips to keep in mind:

1. Gear up:
    - Choose a bike suitable for long-distance cycling, like a touring or hybrid bike with comfortable geometry.
    - Always wear a properly fitting helmet to protect your head in case of accidents.
    - Carry a basic repair kit with essentials like spare tubes, tire levers, a pump, and tools for on-the-go repairs.

2. Maintenance matters:
    - Before setting off on your adventure, thoroughly inspect your bike to ensure everything is in good condition – brakes, gears, and tires included.
    - Keep the chain well-lubricated to enhance performance and prevent wear.

3. Safety first:
    - Stay aware of traffic rules and road conditions throughout your journey. Whenever possible, stick to designated paths and follow local cycling regulations.
    - Increase your visibility by wearing bright reflective clothing, especially during low-light conditions. Equip your bike with front and rear lights as well.

4. Renting options:
    - If you don't have your own bike, there are several local businesses along the Alpe Adria Cycle Path that offer rental services. Make sure to choose a reputable provider with well-maintained bikes.
    - During peak seasons, it's advisable to book your rental bike in advance to secure availability.

5. Cyclist-friendly services:

- Look for accommodations that specifically cater to cyclists. These places often provide secure bike storage facilities along with repair tools and laundry services.

- Explore transportation options that accommodate cyclists such as trains with dedicated bike compartments or bike-friendly shuttles.

6. Navigate with ease:

- Consider using GPS devices or smartphone apps with reliable offline maps to navigate the route effortlessly.

- Follow the official Alpe Adria Cycle Path signage to ensure you stay on the right track.

7. Stay fueled and hydrated:

- Carry a reusable water bottle to stay hydrated throughout your ride. Identify water refill stations along the route and plan accordingly.

- Pack nutrient-rich snacks like trail mix, energy bars, and fruits to keep your energy levels up during the journey.

8. Weather-ready:

- Be prepared for changing weather conditions by wearing layered clothing. Check the weather forecast before you start and pack accordingly.

- Don't forget to carry a lightweight, waterproof jacket in case of unexpected rain.

9. Emergency preparedness:

- Save local emergency numbers and contacts in your phone before you embark on your journey. Familiarize yourself with nearby medical facilities and repair shops.

- It's also a good idea to carry a basic first aid kit with essentials like bandages, pain relievers, and any personal medications.

Cycling along the Alpe Adria Cycle Path is an incredible adventure through the heart of Europe. By prioritizing safety, staying well-prepared, and embracing the stunning landscapes along the way, you'll create unforgettable memories on this remarkable journey.

Detailed Route Descriptions for the Alpe Adria Cycle Path

Planning a cycling adventure along the Alpe Adria Cycle Path? We've got you covered with detailed route descriptions for each section. These descriptions will help you navigate through diverse landscapes, charming towns, and cultural gems, ensuring an unforgettable journey. So let's dive in!

Section 1: Salzburg to Villach

Starting in Salzburg, you'll be captivated by its historic Old Town and the iconic Hohensalzburg Fortress. As you pedal southward, following the Salzach River, picturesque landscapes will unfold before your eyes. Don't miss a stop in Bischofshofen, known for its charming market square. And make sure to take in the beauty of Lake Millstatt as you cycle along its shores. The Drau Cycle Path will then lead you through lush greenery and riverside trails until you reach Villach—a medieval town bursting with charm and vibrancy.

Section 2: Villach to Udine

Leaving Villach behind, prepare to be enchanted by Faaker See—an alpine lake that will leave you breathless with its beauty. The Julian Alps await as you venture further into stunning mountain scenery. Crossing the border from Austria to Italy marks a transition not only in landscapes but also in culture—a true feast for the senses! Pedaling through enchanting Italian villages allows for a full immersion into history and local charm until finally arriving in Udine—a city renowned for its Renaissance architecture and vibrant piazzas.

Section 3: Udine to Grado

Udine's historic center is a must-see on this leg of your journey—medieval squares and ornate architecture await your exploration. As you cycle through the Friuli wine region, vineyard-covered hills create a picturesque backdrop against which memories are made. Reaching the Adriatic coast brings refreshing sea breezes and stunning coastal views that will invigorate your senses. Conclude this section in Grado—a charming island town with a rich maritime history.

Section 4: Grado to Trieste

From Grado's sandy beaches and vibrant atmosphere, embark on a scenic ride along the Gulf of Trieste. The natural beauty of this coastal region is simply breathtaking. Arriving in Trieste, prepare to be immersed in its rich cultural heritage, from Roman ruins to Habsburg-era architecture. Explore the historic center, adorned with elegant squares and historic landmarks that tell tales of times gone by.

These detailed route descriptions provide valuable insights into elevation profiles and difficulty ratings for each section. They'll help you plan your journey effectively, taking into account the varying terrains and highlights along the way. So gear up and get ready for an adventure of a lifetime!

The Alpe Adria Cycle Path not only promises a breathtaking cycling adventure but also provides a unique opportunity to immerse oneself in the vibrant cultural tapestry of the region. To enhance your journey, here is a handpicked calendar featuring local events, festivals, and markets that take place along the route throughout the year. By aligning your trip with these lively celebrations, you can truly experience the essence of this remarkable region.

1. Spring Delights: March to May

April: Fruška Gora Cherry Festival (Near Udine, Italy)

- Embrace the arrival of spring at Udine's Cherry Festival, where the region's delectable cherries take center stage. Indulge in local culinary delights and soak up the festive atmosphere as you mingle with fellow cyclists.

May: Villach May Fair (Villach, Austria)

- Welcome spring with open arms at Villach's May Fair, a delightful celebration complete with traditional music, vibrant parades, and local crafts. Immerse yourself in Austrian culture against the backdrop of picturesque landscapes.

2. Summer Extravaganza: June to August

July: Grado Sea Festival (Grado, Italy)

- As summer reaches its zenith, Grado invites you to join their Sea Festival—a lively tribute to maritime culture. Enjoy seaside festivities accompanied by live music and savor fresh seafood delicacies.

August: Trieste Film Festival (Trieste, Italy)

- Film enthusiasts pedaling through Trieste in August can delight in attending the city's prestigious Film Festival. Immerse yourself in cinematic artistry through enchanting open-air screenings and captivating events.

3. Autumn Harvest: September to November

September: Udine Far East Film Festival (Udine, Italy)

- Experience an intriguing fusion of Asian cinema and Italian culture at Udine's renowned Far East Film Festival. Immerse yourself in the diverse cinematic offerings while exploring the city's enchanting streets.

October: Villach Harvest Festival (Villach, Austria)

- Villach embraces autumn with open arms at its vibrant Harvest Festival—a celebration of regional produce, traditional music, and colorful processions. Delight your taste buds with local flavors as you soak in the festive atmosphere.

4. Winter Wonder: December to February

December: Trieste Christmas Market (Trieste, Italy)

- Let Trieste's magical Christmas Market transport you to a winter wonderland adorned with twinkling lights, festive decorations, and seasonal treats. Embrace the joyous spirit of the season as you explore this enchanting market.

February: Villach Carnival (Villach, Austria)

- Bid farewell to winter in style by joining Villach's exuberant Carnival celebrations in February. Immerse yourself in a world of parades, costumes, and jubilant festivities as you become part of this lively tradition.

This Events and Festivals Calendar adds an extra layer of cultural richness to your Alpe Adria Cycle Path experience. By planning your journey around these vibrant celebrations, you can truly immerse yourself in the diverse traditions and festivities that await you along the route.

Embarking on a cycling adventure along the Alpe Adria Cycle Path offers an opportunity to traverse diverse landscapes and connect with key towns and landmarks. To make the most of your journey, it's crucial to navigate and recognize the vital crossroads that lie ahead. Here's an extensive guide to these pivotal junctions, guaranteeing a seamless and enjoyable cycling experience:

1. Salzburg, Austria - Where It All Begins:
   - Your expedition commences in the captivating city of Salzburg, exuding a blend of historical charm and cultural opulence. This starting point holds significance as you set off from Salzburg Cathedral, an iconic architectural marvel nestled in the heart of the city.

2. Tauern Cycle Path Intersection:
   - As you pedal southward, a notable crossroad appears—the intersection with Tauern Cycle Path. This juncture serves as a pivotal point that allows cyclists to continue their journey towards the sun-kissed southern regions.

3. Villach - Embracing the Drava River:
   - Villach stands as a major hub where the Alpe Adria Cycle Path meets with the majestic Drava River. Take a moment here to relish in the serene ambiance by its riverside while contemplating an enticing detour to explore various attractions within this charming town.

4. Lake Faak am See - A Scenic Diversion:
   - Along your path lies Lake Faak am See—a haven of picturesque beauty that presents itself as an enchanting detour option for nature enthusiasts seeking tranquility amidst stunning vistas. Though not directly on your main route, this scenic lake provides an exquisite diversion well worth experiencing.

5. Klagenfurt - Immersed in Cultural Splendors:
   - Klagenfurt—Carinthia's splendid capital—beckons with a plethora of cultural delights. This junction represents an opportune moment to delve into the city's myriad museums, parks, and bask in the presence of the iconic Lindwurm statue.

6. Rosental Valley - Embracing Nature's Serenity:

- The junction leading to the Rosental Valley unfolds a magnificent retreat into nature's serene embrace. As you cycle through this verdant valley, immerse yourself in its lush landscapes and be charmed by its quaint villages.

7. Udine, Italy - Crossing Borders into Italian Splendor:

- Udine marks a significant border-crossing junction as you enter Italy—a momentous transition both in terms of scenery and culture. Take a pause here to relish this shift and savor the beauty that awaits as you embark on the Italian leg of your journey.

8. Aquileia - A Glimpse into History:

- Aquileia invites you to indulge in a historical interlude as you encounter this notable crossroad along your path. Explore ancient Roman ruins and marvel at the profound historical significance that permeates this region.

9. Grado - Coastal Charms Unveiled:

- The coastal town of Grado unveils itself as an enchanting junction where your path meets the Adriatic Sea. Delight in its coastal charms, frolic on sandy beaches, and immerse yourself in the unique atmosphere that pervades this picturesque town.

10. Muggia - Gateway to Trieste:

- Muggia serves as an alluring gateway before reaching Trieste—the final destination on your cycling odyssey. This charming town provides a prelude to the last leg of your journey while allowing you to revel in captivating coastal allure.

11. Trieste – Where Your Journey Culminates:

- Trieste—the ultimate destination—ushers in the culmination of your Alpe Adria Cycle Path adventure. The various crossroads leading into Trieste guide you towards iconic landmarks such as Piazza Unità d'Italia—an awe-inspiring square where your extraordinary cycling odyssey finds its grand finale.

By familiarizing yourself with these key junctions, you'll elevate your cycling experience, ensuring that you don't overlook the cultural, historical, and natural treasures that grace the Alpe Adria Cycle Path. So hop on your bike, embrace the journey, and enjoy every moment of this remarkable adventure!

Here are some incredible accommodations to consider as you embark on your journey through Austria:

1. Salzburg, Austria - Starting Point:

a. Hotel Sacher Salzburg offers a luxurious experience with its prime location at Schwarzstraße 5-7, 5020 Salzburg, Austria. You can reach them at +43 662 889770 or visit their website [here](https://www.sacher.com/en/hotel-sacher-salzburg/).

b. Experience the grandeur of Sheraton Grand Salzburg located at Auerspergstraße 4, 5020 Salzburg, Austria. For reservations and inquiries, contact them at +43 662 889990 or check out their website [here](https://www.marriott.com/hotels/travel/szgsi-sheraton-grand-salzburg/).

2. Tauern Cycle Path Intersection:

a. Immerse yourself in history and charm at Hotel Steinerwirt 1493 situated on Kitzbüheler Str. 2, 6370 Kitzbühel, Austria. Contact them at +43 5356 66680 or explore more on their website [here](https://www.steinerwirt.com/en/).

b. Indulge in comfort and elegance at Hotel Goldener Greif located on Vorderstadt 7-9, 6370 Kitzbühel, Austria. Feel free to reach out to them at +43 5356 62336 or visit their website [here](https://www.hotel-goldener-greif.at/en/).

3. Villach - Meeting the Drava River:

a. Experience romance and relaxation at Romantik Hotel Post nestled in Hauptplatz 13, 9500 Villach, Austria. You can contact them directly at +43 4242 22522 or visit their website [here](https://www.post-villach.at/en/).

b. Stay at Hotel City located in Hauptplatz 1, 9500 Villach, Austria, and indulge in their exceptional hospitality. For inquiries and reservations, call +43 4242 27844 or check out their website [here](https://www.hotelcity-villach.at/en/).

4. Lake Faak am See - Scenic Detour:

a. Enjoy breathtaking views at Seehotel Astoria situated on Seeuferlandesstraße 59, 9583 Faak am See, Austria. You can contact them at +43 4254 2188 or find out more on their website [here](https://www.astoria-velden.at/en/).

b. Unwind and relax at Hotel Karnerhof located on Karnerhofweg 10, 9580 Drobollach am Faakersee, Austria.

To make a reservation or inquire further, please call +43 4254 21880 or visit their website [here](https://www.karnerhof.com/en/).

5. Klagenfurt - Cultural Interlude:

a. Experience the warm hospitality of Hotel Sandwirth as you explore Klagenfurt located at Pernhartgasse 9,
9020 Klagenfurt, Austria.

For reservations and inquiries, contact them directly at +43 463 56209 or visit their website [here](https://www.sandwirth.at/en/).

b. Immerse yourself in luxury at Hotel Palais Porcia situated in Neuer Platz 13, 9020 Klagenfurt, Austria.

To book your stay or learn more about the hotel's offerings, call +43 463 553660
or visit their website [here](https://www.porcia.at/en/).

6. Lake Klopein - A Haven of Relaxation:

a. Experience pure bliss at Hotel Reichmann, located at Westuferstraße 29, 9122 Sankt Kanzian am Klopeiner See, Austria. To make a reservation, you can contact them at +43 4239 2222. For more information, visit their website [here](https://www.reichmann.co.at/en/).

b. Indulge in tranquility at Hotel Birkenhof am Klopeiner See, situated at Westuferstraße 17, 9122 Sankt Kanzian am Klopeiner See, Austria. To book your stay, feel free to call them at +43 4239 2490 or visit their website [here](https://www.hotel-birkenhof.at/en/).

7. Globasnitz - Crossing the Border to Slovenia:

a. Immerse yourself in the beauty of nature and find comfort at Hotel Kärntner Stub'n located at Marktplatz 6, 9132 Gallizien, Austria. For inquiries and reservations, reach out to them at +43 4237 2232 or explore their website [here](https://www.kaerntnerstubn.at/en/).

b. Discover serenity at Hotel Gril nestled on DSGstraße 2 in the enchanting town of Gallizien (9132), Austria. Give them a call at

+43 4237 5133 or check out their website
[here](https://www.hotel-gril.at/en/) to secure your stay.

8. Pliberk - Unveiling History:

a. Step back in time and immerse yourself in history with a stay at Hotel Schlosswirt situated on Hauptplatz 8 in Maria Rain (9162), Austria. To make a reservation, contact them at +43 4223 2316 or visit their website [here](https://www.schlosswirt-mariarain.at/en/).

b. Experience the charm of the past at Gasthof Kaiser, located on Marktplatz 3 in Maria Rain (9162), Austria. For bookings and inquiries, dial +43 4223 2316 or explore their website [here](https://www.gasthof-kaiser.at/en/).

9. Klagenfurt - A Journey into Culture (Return):

a. Unwind in style at Hotel Sandwirth, situated at Pernhartgasse 9 in Klagenfurt (9020), Austria. To reserve your stay, call them at +43 463 56209 or visit their website [here](https://www.sandwirth.at/en/).

b. Immerse yourself in elegance and sophistication with a stay at Hotel Palais Porcia located on Neuer Platz 13 in Klagenfurt (9020), Austria. Contact them at +43 463 553660 or check out their website [here](https://www.porcia.at/en/) for more information.

10. Grado - Coastal Bliss:

a. Indulge in the beauty of Grado and experience true relaxation at Hotel Savoy, situated on Riva Scaramuzza, 7, Grado GO (34073), Italy. For reservations and inquiries, please call +39 0431 8367 or visit their website [here](https://www.hotelsavoy-grado.it/en/).

b. Discover comfort and tranquility at Hotel Fonzari nestled on Via Marco Polo, 2 in Grado GO (34073), Italy. Feel free to contact them at +39 0431 877888 or explore their website [here](https://www.hotelfonzari.it/en/).

11. Trieste - Journey's End:

a. Savoia Excelsior Palace
   - Located at Riva del Mandracchio, 4, Trieste TS, Italy
   - Contact number: +39 040 77941

   - Visit their website: [Savoia Excelsior Palace](https://www.savoytrieste.it/en/)
   b. Urban Hotel Design
      - Situated at Via Punta del Forno, 3, Trieste TS, Italy
      - Contact number: +39 040 235105
      - Visit their website: [Urban Hotel Design](https://www.urbanhotel.it/en/)

Enhancing your navigation experience on the Alpe Adria Cycle Path can be made more convenient with the help of various mobile navigation apps designed specifically for cyclists. These apps not only provide real-time guidance but also track your progress and offer valuable information about the route. Here are some highly recommended mobile navigation apps that you can consider:

1. Komoot: This app offers a range of features including turn-by-turn voice navigation, offline maps for areas with limited mobile coverage, points of interest along the route, and elevation profiles with difficulty ratings. You can find more information about Komoot on their [website](https://www.komoot.com/).

2. Strava: Strava is another popular app that provides GPS tracking to record your rides. It also has a unique feature called "Segments" which allows you to compete with other cyclists. Additionally, it offers route planning with a heatmap of popular paths and a beacon feature to share your location with friends and family. You can learn more about Strava on their [website](https://www.strava.com/).

3. MapOut: If you prefer interactive offline maps, MapOut is a great choice. It allows customizable route planning, provides elevation profiles and distance markers, and supports importing and exporting GPX files. For more details about MapOut, you can visit their [website](https://www.mapout.app/).

4. Ride with GPS: This app offers turn-by-turn voice navigation as well as offline maps for use without cellular data connectivity. It also provides elevation profiles and ride statistics to help you track your performance. Additionally, Ride with GPS allows users to share their routes within the community. To find out more about Ride with GPS, check out their [website](https://ridewithgps.com/).

5. Google Maps: Known for its detailed maps and extensive coverage, Google Maps is a reliable option for cycling navigation too.It provides turn-by-turn navigation, detailed cycling paths,

offline maps for areas with no data connectivity, and information on nearby services and points of interest. You can access Google Maps through their [website](https://www.google.com/maps).

Before embarking on your cycling adventure along the Alpe Adria Cycle Path, it is advisable to download one or more of these apps to enhance your navigation experience. Remember to keep the apps updated and ensure that you have the necessary offline maps downloaded for uninterrupted guidance throughout your journey.

When embarking on your adventure along the Alpe Adria Cycle Path, it's essential to take advantage of the valuable resources offered by local tourist information centers. These centers provide cyclists with assistance, maps, and insights into the region, ensuring a smooth and enjoyable journey. Let's explore some key information centers along the route:

1. The Salzburg Tourist Information Center is located at Mozartplatz 5, 5020 Salzburg, Austria. You can contact them at +43 662 889870. They offer a range of services including detailed maps of the Alpe Adria Cycle Path, information on local attractions and accommodations, as well as assistance with route planning and logistics.

2. Another important center is Villach Tourismus Information situated at Hauptplatz 1, 9500 Villach, Austria. To reach them, dial +43 4242 2052900. Their services include providing local expertise on the Alpe Adria Cycle Path in the Villach region, offering recommendations for dining options and sightseeing opportunities, and providing brochures and maps specifically designed for cyclists.

3. If you find yourself in Udine UD Italy during your journey, make sure to visit the Udine Tourism Office located at Piazza I° Maggio 8, 33100 Udine UD Italy. They can be reached at +39 0432 1274221. The office offers valuable information regarding the Italian section of the Alpe Adria Cycle Path as well as cultural and historical insights into Udine and its surrounding areas. Additionally, they can assist you with accommodation bookings.

4. In Tarvisio UD Italy lies Tarvisio Tourist Office found at Piazza Unità d'Italia 1, 33018 Tarvisio UD Italy; their contact number is +39 0428 2392. The office provides guidance on cycling routes through the Tarvisio region along with recommendations for outdoor activities and nature experiences. They are also a great source of information on local events and festivals.

5. The Kranjska Gora Tourist Information Centre, situated at Borovška cesta 92e, 4280 Kranjska Gora, Slovenia, is another

valuable resource along the Alpe Adria Cycle Path. You can reach them at +386 4 580 9440. They offer information on the Slovenian segment of the path, suggest outdoor adventure activities and points of interest, as well as provide assistance with transportation and accommodation.

6. Lastly, the Gailtal Tourismus - Hermagor Information center located at Ev.-Karl-Domanig-Platz 4, 9620 Hermagor, Austria can be contacted at +43 4282 3131. They provide local insights into the Gailtal Valley section of the cycle path along with recommendations for traditional cuisine and cultural experiences. Additionally, they have brochures and maps tailored specifically for cyclists.

These tourist information centers are equipped to enhance your Alpe Adria Cycle Path journey by providing you with all the necessary information and support for a memorable cycling experience. Before embarking on your adventure, consider stopping by these centers to get the latest updates and personalized recommendations to make your journey even more enjoyable.

1. Weather Preparedness:
   - Prior to embarking on each leg of your journey, it's crucial to check the weather forecast. The Alpe Adria region boasts diverse climates, so being equipped for possible rain, wind, or sudden temperature fluctuations is paramount.
2. Emergency Contacts:
   - Ensure that you save local emergency numbers in your mobile phone and carry a comprehensive list of essential contacts, including local authorities, medical facilities, and your embassy or consulate.
3. Health and Safety Essentials:
   - Don't forget to pack a basic first aid kit containing items like bandages and pain relievers. Additionally, include any personal medications you may require. Sunscreen, insect repellent, and a refillable water bottle are also indispensable.
4. Currency and Payment Methods:
   - While larger towns may accept credit cards as a form of payment, it's worth noting that smaller establishments and rural areas often prefer cash transactions. It's wise to carry sufficient local currency to handle unforeseen situations.
5. Cultural Etiquette:
   - Take the time to familiarize yourself with the customs and etiquette of each country along the route. Show respect for local traditions, be considerate towards residents you encounter along the way, and adhere to trail regulations.
6. Trail Etiquette:
   - Embrace established trail etiquette practices such as yielding to pedestrians when necessary and notifying others when overtaking them on the path. Showing respect for nature is vital; try to stay on designated paths in order to minimize any potential environmental impact.
7. Accommodation Reservations:

- During peak seasons—especially popular cycling months—it's advisable to book accommodations in advance in order to secure your preferred lodgings without any last-minute hassles.

8. Language Considerations:

   - Make an effort to learn a few basic phrases in the local languages spoken along the route. While English may be widely understood, locals greatly appreciate when visitors engage in their native tongue.

9. Bike Maintenance:

   - Regularly inspect your bicycle for any potential issues, paying special attention to the brakes, tires, and gears. It's beneficial to familiarize yourself with basic bike repair skills or carry information about nearby bike repair shops.

10. Exploring Local Cuisine:

   - Embrace the culinary diversity that awaits you along the route. Be sure to sample local dishes and beverages, and don't hesitate to ask locals or fellow cyclists for recommendations—they often hold valuable insights!

11. Waste Disposal:

   - Show mindfulness towards waste disposal while on the path. Carry a small trash bag with you to collect any litter you encounter and dispose of it responsibly in designated bins.

12. Navigation Aids:

   - While digital maps and GPS are undoubtedly convenient, having a physical map can prove beneficial—particularly in areas where connectivity is limited. Additionally, ensure that your navigation devices are fully charged before setting off on your journey.

13. Rest and Recovery:

   - Listen attentively to your body's needs and schedule rest days whenever necessary. Prioritizing adequate sleep, hydration, and stretching will contribute significantly to an enjoyable cycling experience free from injuries.

14. Trail Stories and Recommendations:

   - Engage with fellow cyclists and locals along the way; their trail stories and recommendations can add a personal touch to your journey while potentially leading you towards hidden gems waiting to be discovered.

By incorporating these additional tips into your Alpe Adria Cycle Path adventure, you'll enhance both the smoothness of your journey as well as its enriching nature—allowing you ample opportunity to relish in the awe-inspiring landscapes and cultural treasures that await you along the route.

www.ingramcontent.com/pod-product-compliance
Lightning Source LLC
LaVergne TN
LVHW050542200726
843506LV00001B/71